Abhay Vasudeva

Abhayvasudev2425@gmail.com

Eternal Emotions
By ABHAY VASUDEV

Welcome to the imperfect book

(simple words but deep meaning)

© 2025 [ABHAY VASUDEV]. All Rights Reserved.

Disclaimer (people who can feel, only able to read)

Dedication (Thanks to my heart for expressing emotions)

Some words……

All the emotions that messed up inside my heart, I turned
to poetry because I believed that true emotions cannot be
shown completely, but we can express them in poetry…

Abhay….

First Emotion

Deserve love,

Where emotions engulf like cosmic tides.

But love in my heart already vanishes,

Which was more valuable than life,

Now my heart begins to shrink,

Tears that I ingest,

The body survives, but the soul is in a cage,

Solitude and clouds of sorrow covered me,

Bathed in the moon's pale glow,

I weep alone,

Wandering in the streets till midnight,

Then suddenly saw your text,

Staying on the exact path where you left,

Once you filled me with love,

now I feel just numb,

Part of me is incomplete now,

You are gone,

In your arms, my heart reclaims its home.

Ocean's devotion

Do you remember that day,
when you vowed to love me till I die?
I gazed at you in a way,
That no one could ever imagine,
I held your hand so gently,
You felt like heaven in my grasp,
Staring at the endless ocean,
Even when you stood on the distant shore,
I still saw you with my heart's devotion.
I could feel your presence near,
If you called my name,
I'd swim through the ocean's depths, my dear,
Even if I were to drown in its frame,
My soul would find its way to you,
Just wait for me a little while,
Look in the direction where love grew,
where my heart paused and found its smile.

If you asked me to wait,
I'd stand through all the seasons that pass,
Till the ocean's waters abate,
Till the birds in the sky amass,
I'd always remain in your sight,
For you, I'd cross a broken bridge's span,
Even in its dim light, It's
all about you, understand.
How can I explain these feelings so deep,
how can I express my heartfelt fiction?
Pain has become my silent keeper,
There's no cure for my addiction,
Except for your loving hold,
Surviving without you is hard to
conceive. In your arms, my story
unfolds, In your love, I truly
believe.

Moonlit longing

Summer passes away but memories are frozen,
How could I imagine my lonely nights,
I never chosen
we used to talk, lying on the grass
Stars were our home,
Now moon is the way of communication,
Watching sunset and sunrise,
Distance from miles,
Silence but on mind your voices,
Tears become ocean,
Drowning in scars,
life feels incomplete,
Teach me how to live, find my own beat,
In this void, show me a new way to thrive,
Guide me through a soulless life,
Cannot find peace to fill
Because only you I believe in,
Give me the love,
Which I'm waiting for,
Which I'm wandering for.

Glimpse of you

Counting stars, it's just lovers' things,
If you say, for you, the whole universe I can bring,
Be my Saturn, and I will be your ring,
Be my instrument, I be your tune,
You and I are like guitar strings,
Connected but has distance,
My heart belongs to you without reason,
Thinking of you in every season,
It's just you and for you my feelings,
I wish it would be you, I our home,
Every morning I make some toast,
Every night for you, I write poetry in notes,
Lying on the grass,
We would count stars,
It's just my dream,
Your glimpse I see,
Your voice I hear,
Never met you in real that's the twist,
Without you, Little lost, little grown,
Whatever it is, without you, I'm always going to feel alone...

Unseen universe

My heart cannot beat if I don't think,
About you,
My eyes would not blink,
After it's unable to recognize you,
The flower which you plucked,
And thrown to the ocean,
Not drowning, not swimming,
Just withering,
My life is yours,
How do I make a walk with smile?
When you are not in my path,
I'm unable to see the blue sky,
Because it's in your eyes,
you're not able to hear,
Because you are my ears,
Millions of people, but they are invisible,
But I can see you even if you are in another universe,
The ocean will be dry,
Then I don't need to survive,
because I will mix in the ocean and vanish.
I tried to hold your hand,
But It felt like I was holding sand,
waves washed it away.
In my heart it's fixed so here you always stay.

LOST

I'm just lost,
Smiling but I'm Dysthymic,
Have no one or I'm misfits in the puzzle,
Stuck inside in my own, thoughts always living like a Solivagant ,
Don't know the reason why God make me like this,
Having Nostomania, feeling is miserabilist,
Someday just like a story I would to finish,
Without end, just with sadness,
With dread words, writing about pain,
How do I let it go,
It's the last thing which I have,
Just like a deep connection between brush and paints,
I write your name, and wish you show up,
It would be insane, without clouds it would be rain,
In summer's my heart still feel cold,
If you would not come and my hand you would hold..

Journey of love

I asked Rain to take me,
Drop me in the holy place,
Where I will see you,
Wind will guide me on the path,
Clouds become my transport,
Your love shields me from lightning's fright,
To reach my destiny,
Which leads me to you,
Which ends after meeting you,
At the fair, our hands intertwined, Blessings
showered, and the world aligned.

Sometimes we end up in grave without getting flowers in funerals

Unseen longings

I don't know how many times I open our chat,

To send texts, but in my heart, there's nothing left.

Lost within the universe,

Trying to escape this world's curse.

To meet you in the next life, I anticipate,

Hold me while I have to wait.

I will see you one day; this is my faith,

Wherever I go, it doesn't matter,

At the end of the road, by the end of my hope,

You're the one I still long for,

Heartbreaks and tears that pour,

Mend me with your presence, even if it's

slow, Even if the earth burns to the ground

below, Just let me be around, I implore. I'll

weave you into every story I create, I write

so my feelings never dissipate.

But, what's the point of writing if you never read?

What's the point of feeling if you never heed?

The value of my heart is nothing if you can't take it,

In the pages of my words, I'll wait for you, for eternity.

Unbroken longing

Even if I die,

My love will remain alive,

I'm broken stars,

Only pain continues to thrive,

In your love, I remained deceived,

Just tell me why these distances exist,

How can I forget? It's a compulsion,

How do I look at someone else?

When it's still just my imagination that you're with me,

How do I keep my feelings suppressed?

There isn't a folder for your pictures; it's closed,

Feeling lonely and screaming inside,

So that no one hears,

Giving myself false hope that one day you'll come,

My heart is on burning fire,

A love so unrequited, it burns like a pyre,

Without you, I say I'm fine, but I'm a great liar,

After you, only fears are left,

I'm wrapped in my love, holding your memories so tight,

Everything is just lost, I'm wandering in the pain,

It's hard to breathe,

Just hoping you'll come and hold me,

And sit around me...

Unfulfilled yearning

I saw your face in the story today,
After a long time, my hope did sway,
Realizing you're no longer mine,
Living without you, what kind of life is it?
I made a mistake by sending you away from me,
Now time feels like it's crawling for you to see,
Like we used to talk in times gone by.
Now I spend my nights without you, oh so high,
In every thought of mine, you're there, it's true,
You've become ingrained in my mind, it's you,
All that occupies my thoughts, you're the sign.
The time I spent with you, I wish to rewind,
Just want to be yours, and you be mine,
My tears can't express how much I yearn,
My words can't convey the love for which I burn,
My heart longs to hear you in every line.
Come from somewhere, through a window divine,
Melt into the air, touch my heart, be mine,
When I see you smile, I feel so kind,
But what if you'll never be mine?

Unanswered love

I couldn't express the feelings of my heart to you,
How do I convey that these were your promises
too? You drifted away like the wind, so fast,
In the river of your memories, I'm cast. I'm
just a traveller, you're my destination, Hold
my hand, so I find no separation.
Every time your magic fills the rain,
It's just your absence that brings me pain,
Please understand the ache within,
You're my night and my morning's grin,
The reason for my heart's sorrow,
Just writing about you, tomorrow and tomorrow.
Does my love hold no value to you?
Can't you answer my love, tell me what's true?
Asking the clouds about you,
In their shapes, they reveal what's due.
You don't know what you mean to me,
The sole path of my dreams, the key.
When someone asks about love's art,
You were the one who occupied my heart.
What should I do after you're gone?
Counting stars through the night, I carry on,
Missing our talks and the moments we've known.

Capturing your smile

How can mere words capture the magic of your smile?

Thinking about what I should write for a while,

Because every word, every line, is not enough,

The girl of my dreams, it's you, my love.

(keep you in my heart if it's on me.

show some mercy on me

come one time.

Come from my phone screen, let's erase the glass,

Hug me and let our hearts amass.

The vibe I get,

Feels like you're the best I've ever met,

The care you show,

The love you give me, I want it to grow.

I want this forever,

Just promise to leave me never,

Live in my mind and in my dreams,

Hold my hand and love me, it seems,

Let's see the world,

Just come close, my heart is unfurled,

I'm coming with a rose for my rose.

Echoes of love

I don't miss you,

Surrounded by your voice, it's true,

Your memories linger all around,

The whisper of your echoes, a comforting sound,

Still with me, you stay,

Your image in my mind, night and day,

The love within my heart, only you can find,

Wherever I go, you're carried in my soul, entwined.

Come back before I say goodbye,

The clouds in the sky may cry,

But sunlight dries my tears,

My heart's rhythm, fading, my fears.

Hope's echoes slowly grow weak,

You're gone, it's hard to speak.

A secret hope, where words turn silent,

Standing in the rain, I remain patient,

Waiting for you to be my shelter,

In the rain, I'll stay, a love swelter.

You used to call me even without a phone,

Amidst the storm, your absence is known,

Yet your playlist's embrace helps me heal,

The playlist, once our love, a time so surreal.

It's 6 hours and 56 minutes long,

Each song, a memory, where our love belonged.

But that playlist now sits untouched,

For memories of you, a bit too much...

Whispers of Absence

The road now softly whispers, asking where you've gone,

I smile, gaze at the stars; your memory lingers on.

I lay beneath the night sky's vast embrace,

Our echoes surround, in this tranquil space.

Drifting into dreams, I find you there,

Watching a TV show, in a world so fair.

I make you laugh, guarding against life's strife,

As the sun sets down,

Sitting without you on my own,

Each passing moment, I miss you more,

It's a constant ache, deep in my core.

Everything seems fine,

But in your absence, it's hard to survive.

Where are you now? That's what I'm fearing.

I write anew, words meant for just us two,

Though they may not capture all I feel for you,

My words are my solace, a love that's true.

I write for me but always talk about you,

I'm blind, but I can see you so clear,

In your absence, my world's full of fears.

Amid shattered dreams, I strive to create,

A world where your essence, every path does permeate.

I lend your voice to everything I hear,

Listening on repeat, trying to keep you near.

Without you, this world's not my abode,

I'll shatter its silence, walk a lonely road.

I can fight with the whole world,

If you cheer me up,

But how would I fight,

If you tear me up,

For I only yearn to see you by my side,

Just arrive,

In my dreams and become my bride,

In your absence, it's hard to survive...

Echoes of Suffering

My mind filled with black light,

Flowers cutting into my heart,

Like thorns,

Happiness is already gone,

Darkness growling in the dark,

Dreams are already dead,

It's just one life that is hopeless,

It's just one heart that is wrecked,

Maybe I deserve pain,

Without any sins,

The glory of my soul has vanished with daylight,

Complex feelings,

But still leading to a miserable life,

Amidst the moments,

There is silence,

Pain blooms and thrives,

I'll remain in this world, just like this,

Leaking only with the weight of sorrow,

I know you're already gone,

I know you've already faded,

But how did love turn into pain,

How did happiness start kill?

LONELINESS IS THE PART OF EMOTIONS

In the Silence, My Strength

"Whom do I talk to whenever I drown in the dark?

Whom do I share my feelings with

when anxiety is killing, feelings

like no one really cares?

The feelings inside me are buried in the deep layer.

Even if I know all languages,

I still cannot express the pain I feel.

In the shadows of my thoughts,

I search for a glimmer of light.

Hands shake whenever I feel something,

staying up late,

feels like I will die soon.

From morning to night, evening to noon,

just covered with hope about you.

The poison I want to taste,

I mean the pain,

feels like I cannot digest.

Demons seem righteous,

what if I cut my hand?

what if I drown somewhere deep?

Under attack, my soul cannot even scream.

Let me get the peace when the sound of my heart beeps,

stop slowly on repeat.

In the silence of the night, I find my strength anew….

Breathe Without You

Suffering every day just to get to you,

Dying to hear that melodic voice,

After listening, I can die in peace because it's hard to feel.

One rope or cut would be enough, To

let go of the thousands of bleeding wounds,

Which are in my chest, making it hard to breathe.

Trauma makes me hopeless,

The love I gave, that's only God blessed.

In my brain, it's dark, and everything is messed,

I can see a man with an axe wearing a black dress.

My soul is despondent,

Ghosts of nights ask about you,

Trying to hurt me,

So I can give my soul for free.

In my eyes, your face they only can see,

But still, it's all without you,

So hard I can breathe,

Beyond my thoughts, you are somewhere,

Loving you till I die, I swear.

How can I love someone when all I can think about is you?

When I feel only you, when I see only you,

Without you, the count of my life left is few.

Colours of Longing

The colour of every hue reminds me of the colour of your eyes.

Every word, every line, every sentence,

I just write about you.

With eyes shut tight, I glimpse your visage, fair.

In dreams, I find solace; by your side, we share.

Even loving you hurts me

sometimes, But it's the reason

why I'm alive. I stay silent and

feel alone, Until you come

home.

Whenever I write, the misery - I'm not the only one who feels,

But my words bleed.

On every page, your smile holds me.

My ears are suffering,

To hear your melody.

Nights feel interminable when I'm alone,

Heart is longing for your touch,

Soul is screaming, head just bursting

I want to get lost in this sky just like kites, I am jealous

Verses of Longing

Whenever I see that cutest smile,

It gives me peace as well as kills me from inside.

In the moonlight's gentle embrace,

Your memory shines, a comforting grace.

Overthinking covers my heart,

I did everything, but why are you still not here with me tonight?

Through the starry nights and endless skies,

Your absence, a void, in my heart lies.

How can I not love you,

When you are in my mind from wake to bedtime?

Without you, it's impossible to not feel sad.

With every sunrise, hope renews,

That one day, my love, I'll be with you.

Let me know how I will get your love,

Even if we don't talk, I still put you above.

I can forget my face but not yours,

I can hide my pain to make you feel good.

I can forget my voice but not yours,

You don't miss me I hope it's just rumours.

Waiting for you, why is it forever?

Why cannot we give one chance to each other?

Though distance separates, our souls remain entwined,

In the dim light that forever lingers by my side.

Lying down alone and feeling miserable,

My love, a flame that won't subside.

Heart's Echoes

Whenever you text, there's something

I feel in my chest,

Maybe it's my heart calling you,

Or maybe I'm just yearning, yet it's more than a feeling.

Listening to music, but your voice waves in my brain,

Winter's coming, the season of feelings,

I'm not only loving you but also living.

If I were to sell my single memory of you in an auction,

It would remain unsold,

Because it's priceless and shines brighter than gold.

Through life's storms and darkest night,

My love for you shines forever bright.

No one knows the pain,

When I have to love you from heart to veins.

The agony of your absence whispers in my brain,

Yet, in my heart, your love will always remain…

Amber Whispers

Are you watching?

I stay true to my promise,

Even if you departed,

Your memories, a soothing tonic,

My heart beats in harmony,

Tears fall like rain in a world so hypnotic,

Just want to conceal you in my secrets.

Every word I utter is about you,

Feelings uncovered by my demons,

Wandering through your alley,

Screaming but not healing, crying but not flying,

Drowning and not waking up,

Until you appeared at the end of my suffering.

Amber leaves whisper tales of your name,

In the autumn glow, as the season begins to wane,

Shadows of your memories become my friend,

In the deep end, when I'm lost,

I need your light to give me hope.

Galactic Gems of Love

Many diamonds in the universe,

But your smile shines above,

The glory in your eyes,

Gives me butterflies.

Seeing you is my therapy,

Feeling happy,

Whenever I see your text,

The pain that was in my heart has left.

The camera doesn't have the quality

To capture the beauty that only I can see.

In your gaze, my dreams come alive,

In your laughter, my heart takes a dive.

With you forever, I hope to survive…

Solitude's Echo"

Have one thought,

What if I had no emotions,

What if you never came and never left,

Every morning, before opening my eyes,

Have some words in my mind,

Thinking of you,

What if you were always here by my side,

Your absence is my anguish; only pain is my experience.

In the world of sorrow, I'm finding some love,

In addressing the sun,

I'm looking for the evening,

In addressing the moon,

I'm looking for you.

Walking in heaven, your name whispers all around,

There I want to shout,

But my words are silent,

Finding my voice is my task.

Any path I walk, and any place I go,

Only you are my home's door,

You are the voice of my words,

You are the cure for my every scar.

November's Solitude"

In the Month of November,

The view of the heart is still tremendous.

During the night, feelings are trembling,

During the days, demons hide under the bed.

During sunset, you and my emotions met,

The ocean is not wet,

Sand is not dry,

Tears in my eyes, even if I do cry.

Life's just a mess,

You said I'm strong,

I will forget about all of our memories,

Illuminating darkness, our sorrows interlace,

But you were wrong, you are gone,

I'm waiting for you alone, in my home.

I lost count of the days,

I speak, but my words bleed, Writing

about you while my hands incessantly shake,

Going to pretend like I'm happy even when I smile fake.

Month of November,

Here I am on my own....

Change is very important for growth
No one is perfect and neither is my book.

Rewrite story

I wish I could restart my story,

Cause I'm dying so slowly,

I'm lying on a crowded road,

Trying to go back,

Trying to cover my body with rope,

So I could breathe one last time just for a little hope,

This could be the end of everything,

Let's just go somewhere only we know,

Cause I don't let you go,

I lost count after you left me feeling low,

You are already in joy,

It hurts when someone leaves without saying goodbye,

Should I do the same?

My body is craving to cut my hand veins,

Just let my soul free,

Give my body freedom to this pain....

Pain gives us a sixth sense to feel other emotions.

Prayers

I prayed to God to make her mine forever

That's why she left and stayed in my words forever,

You are my once-in-a-lifetime,

I don't know what to say,

So why can't you be mine?

I don't know what I should say,

I tried with every word, but still, it was few,

If you say I can die for you, or if you say I can cry for you,

Would you see me?

Every word I write about you would you read it,

Would you listen to my heartbeat?

Maybe you don't want to understand

Why I'm so cursed,

Maybe I do anything for you but you don't give me a chance,

But still, I hope one day you will meet me,

But still, I hope a day you will hold me,

But still, I hope one day my poetry you would read,

I could get victory on world but if you don't with me it's my biggest defeat

Why won't you open your heart's eyes,

All I ask is just to love me...

MAGICIAN

I might be a magician with words,

But I've lost the feeling of receiving the love, I deserved,

Moon doesn't know the beauty of his own,

Without you, I'm just an incomplete consolation,

Your happiness matters to me

even if it means you have to stay away from yourself,

I tore all of the photos in front of you,

When you left, I collected each piece, mending it with my tears,

Nothing is more beautiful than moonlight and your shine,

Whenever I close my eyes I feel like without you I will never be fine,

Whenever you come into my thoughts I always try to hold it for a while,

Maybe forever, your face I have to hide inside

My soul is buried within your memories,

All I remember is our full-day talks sometimes calls,

I still have our call records on my phone,

Specific folder of your pictures with a pin lock,

Your beautiful voice Is my favorite,

Just wanted to become like rain,

So I can fall on you and heal all your scars,

Let's just talk,

be my wind so I can be your clouds,

During my last breath, I just want to hold you,

During my last blink, I want to see you...

LONGING

In memories of you, I'm los tmyself and

found you,

Every detail etched, forever bound.

Our conversations, now a distant past,

Leave me yearning for a love that will forever last.

I long to hold your hand, to dance in rain,

To lie with you in dry grass, feeling love's sweet pain.

I'd weave a crown of grass leaves, kneel by your side,

And offer you my heart, where love will be our guide.

But now, all efforts seem in vain,

Clouds that once held promise, faded, leaving only

pain. Yet, in the cold air, I still feel your gentle

touch, The last drop of rain, a memory I clutch.

If you ever need me, just a phone call away,

I'll be here, waiting, night and day. For I

thought our love would forever shine, A flame

that burns bright, a love divine. But you took

the coal, leaving only ash and pain, And now,

I'm left to whisper your name in vain.

My heart, once full of hope, now shattered and worn,

My smile, a fleeting memory, a joy that's lost and

torn. Without you, I'm a path that's lost its way,

A hollow body, empty, night and day.

You were my guiding light, my shining star,

Without you, I'm but a shadow, near and far.

RAINBOW

The color of the rainbow,

There is nothing in front of the color of your eyes,

I feel so alive,

When in your eyes, I dive,

When in my imaginary world, I'm holding your hands,

In my fiction, you are mine,

So just listen to me and let's do dance,

The snowfall makes it romantic,

I just want to see you forever, even if I have to buy the ticket,

From God, from my lord,

My destiny would be lost,

If I had never walked towards you,

So just come close and let me hold you from the waist,

Just look's each other eyes and smile on faces,

I can hear your fragrance from miles,

I want to express your heart's beauty, but with words i cannot describe.

So just look at the mirror, you will see crystal clear,

Or just close your eyes and look at the beautiful light which is deep
inside,

Time will be freeze,

When together we breathe,

The relation of you and I, it's

unique, even don't talk for weeks,

still care about how other one

feels...

Love's Ember

Four years ago, you were right here,

My heart beats for you, my love, sincerely.

But now you're gone, and I'm lost in the haze,

My heart cries tears, though the world's amazed.

Do you remember that tender night,

When I shared my feelings, bathed in starlight?

I told you that you filled my empty nights,

And my love for you burned with fiery lights.

We were dancing, and around us there were fireflies,

18th October, freezing weather,

Stars were glowing and gave us a sign to begin together,

Two hearts entwined, under a starry sky forever,

Time passed, and here I'm on my own,

Shouting your name so Loud,

Another poem begins to be completed,

My longing is ongoing,

Your presence is frozen in my mind,

Every cell in my body is yours, I just realized,

Last October was evidence of your extinction,

Now, without you, everything is different,

Though you're gone, my love for you remains eternal,

A flickering flame that will forever burn...

HOLD ME TIGHT

I was depressed,

All in my head everything was just messed,

You showed care and gave hand to hold,

Lift me up from darkness,

Now just stay here always,

Do not know how to remove the distance soon,

Be my reality from my fiction,

In this world nothing is left, to get

Because you I already met,

Will you still stay even I'm the dumbest?

Didn't know what peace was until you I met,

You've shown me the true meaning of tranquillity,

Listen to my silence,

Our bond is like an unspoken melody,

Every phrases of time it's calling you,

Just wait for me and be with me,

I will show you how beautiful you are,

In your eyes, I see the universe's secrets unfold,

Time always flies so just hold me tight,

Show me your love, just give me little hug.

FADING PATH

Letting you go,

Shattering my soul,

Paralyzed, bound to this chair,

Tears drained, I'm hollow, I yearn to hold you,

But my hands won't stir,

I seek dreams of you,

Yet nightmares persist in a blur.

Searching for the love I truly deserve,

In every universe, you I preserve,

Stars guiding, but the path fades,

A void, this connection cascades,

Thought I'd reach you, but I was wrong,

My vivid imagination deceived me all along.

Mention not your name,

Whispers of love come with rain,

I weep when no one's near,

Tears, they hold no value, I fear,

My efforts, futile and undone,

Love's elusive, for the chosen one...

EMPTY ROADS

Empty roads and lonely nights,

Feeling blue,

This feeling isn't new,

If you ask me how I am,

Will Tell you I'm good,

If I don't even eat food,

Pain coming from everywhere,

Without you, my heart is wrecked,

But I'm fine, I swear,

Just on heart little Crack,

Bleeding blue blood,

Drowning in the flood of sorrow,

Your words pierced my heart,

If you want to see how much I love you,

Dig my heart with Harrow,

Without you scared to fall from heights,

Empty roads and lonely nights...

Even if you fail, still try again and again …

FALLING STAR

Dead or alive, your heart never cares about me,

Every day, trying to write few words for you in the shape of poetry,

So you can read, might feel,

Every night there is a storm inside me,

I sleep every day but don't dream,

My eyes can see anything but it's not you so it's always bleeding,

In the clouds, I would write your name,

So it would rain and hide your tears,

because with you I'm not there,

It's been a million years in my head since

we last talked,

It's been years I'm still fucked up,

Memories are on hold,

Time seems sad,

What should I write now when the sound of tears?

You never heard,

I wrote the postcards for you, which were never delivered because I
never sent.

My words filled with dust,

Because you never understood,

What should I do now? Because writing now with the blood of my heart,

It's foggy, my eyes cannot see

anything, maybe it's

darkness, Why you are far?

Just like the broken star I'm falling and burning from inside,

Nobody even I don't care if I'm dead or alive....

Echoes of Absence

I structured a statue in your absence made of your memories,

Many people can love you,

But how they can get a spark in their eyes like me,

How are they going to write your name in their hearts?

Even my shadow is finding your shelter to mix it with you...

Everyone is wandering to see that girl,

Who they felt in my words,

How to tell them that she left me with millions of cuts,

You took with yourself permission to say those magical three words,

The absence in my wounds only can help with the name of love,

Nothings left,

All empty even the darkness already left,

It's just all depression all aggression, loneliness is my addiction and

everything else looks like just fiction,

Sometimes wish clouds would drop some acid,

So I can wash my heart,

Ripped it from my chest and threw it so far,

Every time I look at my own eyes,

Only I can see the sky and the lonely tree,

Which lost all leaves and became dry even roots covered the ocean,

In the barren expanse of my soul,

echoes the silent plea for a drop of solace to quench this endless
drought...

APART

In the shadows of the day, I live with an ache in my heart.

I'm just mess in the dark,

Without you, I feel lost and torn apart.

You came into my life, occupying my soul.

Now, I sit alone, contemplating while my eyes,

search for your presence beyond my control.

In your streets, in your fragrance, I try to immerse.

At night, in a closed room , I witness

memories of you, like a melancholic verse.

Perhaps you have moved on, far away from my sight.

But why didn't you turn back to see my plight?

Why didn't you ask about my State?

Every day, I pray for your happiness and await.

Yet, your eyes never shed a tear.

Time has its say now, and the truth is clear.

You're not here, but I still stand.

In a silent night and rain from above, hand in hand.

Dreams shattered, along with a broken heart.

Feeling the pain, as we remain apart,

Try to smile,

But afraid to cry again, try

to love,

But afraid to die again.

Love is pain, a sweet poison, when we want to die,that desire.

UNEXPECTED

Even our meeting was so unexpected,

I vividly remember, when we saw each other for the first time,

You literally laughed and I gave a little smile,

Even you live a little far little close,

Just chant my name whenever you feel sad,

I'm here to take away your scars and make you feel fine,

If you say I will shade the sky with your favourite color,

So can I be your lover?

I feel like we made it for each other,

Even on the bus, your smile melts my heart,

Took my breath away from my chest,

I think for you I'm the best,

If you say I will take all of your pain,

If you say I will hold your hands and never let it fade away,

So just stay,

Be mine, hold me so tight,

Just turn off the light,

Let's dream together even if it's day or night, In

the embrace of your love, I find my solace bright,

Together, hand in hand, we'll paint our forever, our eternal light.

The Darkest Nights

In the darkest nights,

I don't even see Arcturus, Spica and Vega, (stars name)

Darkness becomes the mega,

Half-moon,

Emptiness on my heart,

Among Dark clouds and whispering of trees,

Crying on my knees,

Glistening eyes, tears turned to embrace,

Forever echoes the second name of pain,

Don't recognize myself in the dark,

Lost in shadows, searching for a spark,

The Trauma from past,

Fixed with my spirit,

In my every single breath,

In my chest, I feel a hidden wire's sting,

Unveiling my pain, it begins to sing,

Amidst agony's grasp, I strive to find.

Love's Curse

You didn't stay here,

So be with my memories forever,

Never want to fade away from your presence,

Your words cut me deep and impossible to heal,

Holding the hope, one day you look in my eyes,

See all of my love that left after my blood dropped,

One day you will see that my love for you I never stopped,

I'm addicted to love you, it's the curse,

Not going away not staying,

I am young age but in the love world I'm the oldest,

Even though I'm not smart in the love world I'm the son of a goddess,

With everyone, I talked about you,

Told everyone that you are my world,

Now they laughed, how she's let me down,

Trying to live alone, so in the memories I can be with her,

Don't want to stay, don't want to go anywhere,

Don't want to live anymore, don't want to die,

Just want to feel something little more....

Timeless Melody

If home is a person,

For me it should be you,

For everyone If there is only one tree,

You are the tree for me,

I wish you would be a dream,

Which I see every night,

I wish in the sky your face would print,

So I can see anywhere I go,

At night it touches me becoming snow,

I wish you would be the answer of my all questions,

I wish I put your picture with God and you be my devotion,

I wish you be my time so I always wear watch,

Or my home would made with clock's,

In this cold world, be my warm home,

Whenever I'm with you, feels like deja vu,

Maybe in every life there is always you and I,

Thinking about you if it's a crime, I would give my heart to you as a fine.....

GRAVE

Looking at the wall of my room,

A heart immersed in trauma,

blood's haunting dance,

Dying everyday but breathing,

Soul wandering in hell,

Pain, my eternal companion,

transforms into an unwavering line of growth,

In your absence,

I yearn to call you near,

But alas, my voice cannot reach your ear,

Fear courses through each breath I take,

As pain's melody echoes,

a haunting ache,

A painful smile,

sorrow dry as the desert sand,

Closing eyes,

Dreaming laying in the grave...

Sometimes only regret left inside us...

VOICE

My eyes are closed,

But your face is still in front of me,

I sat down and tried to think,

Without you I just over think,

Our first song tuning around my head,

Looking at the wall while lying down on the bed,

Where your pictures are painted on the wall,

A silent voice, cannot express what's going on,

You just slipped away,

I put a fake smile on my face,

I am intimidated by not feeling that love again,

But whenever I see you,

This idea always fails,

Didn't know this pain,

Before choosing you every day again and again,

How could I imagine you breaking my heart,?

I'm just a mess in the dark,

I'm just anxious and living too far,

Without you, it's like night without stars,

what if you met someone?

What if my life doesn't begin?

Without you, it's incomplete and wasted,

What if I wasn't done loving you,

What if my heart only looking for you?
What if you are the mirror of love,
Which I want front of my face,
All your memories I cannot erase,
what if I would never run away,
Will you chase me?
Will you come to see me?
Will you stand and put flowers on my grave?
you are the only one who's my favourite...

Pieces of My Heart

My ears are bleeding,

Cause the remaining voice of you inside me its fading,

In the echoes of silence, your presence remains,

I feel pain in my chest when someone says your name,

Why am I not enough?

Lost in memories of the river,

A dance of shadows and light,

To release my stress,

Whispers of your name linger in the night's embrace,

In your arms, I want to rest,

Living in opposite directions,

No one is close to me,

Even I laugh with people when they're around,

Searching for solace in the stars' gentle glow,

Life, tell me why you're mad at me,

Why you left me drowning,

Just breathing, is it a crime?

Just loving you, it's infinite,

Take me back to the time,

Take me back when you were mine,

Before my mind starts to wonder,

Pieces of my heart are a hundred,

Promises I made which are unbreakable,

Even though you went, I'm still following your path…

Only your heart cares about what you feel.

Not others…

Love or nature

Nature is quiet,

It's raining, birds are singing,

Clouds are completely merged,

It's monsoon,

A Romantic day, yet I sit alone,

Imagining us, sipping tea with a romantic backdrop,

You wrapped in my arms,

Your warmth erases all my scars,

Suddenly, my eyes open, and it's all dark,

Tea becomes cold,

Your head is no longer on my shoulder,

Thunder and lightning,

I'm all alone without you at home,

I scream by looking at the sky,

Winds playing a sad tune,

My heart burned without fuel,

I cried all the tears fell on the ground,

I put my face above the fire,

So I can imagine you giving me warmth,

I'm lost in a storm of lament,

Sombre before I closed my eyes,

Then saw your face bathed in the daylight.

Distance

Talks between Me and my soul,

Distance is just like December to January,

Just like a heart, I'm all alone,

Incomplete just like February,

Writing about feelings,

Does anyone care?

People wearing layers on their hearts,

Smile is a makeup for hiding scares,

Whenever I take a step,

Don't know why thrones fall from clouds,

Trying to sleep, but suddenly it's morning,

Leave me, it's easy, just say you're sorry,

If I'm wood, it would be hollow,

If I'm room, it would be empty,

If I'm something, I would be cursed,

In the daylight, I would be a shadow,

Trying to see the whole world,

But stuck inside a cage, a maze,

Wish I were someone's story,

So someone would read to me daily,

Wish I were someone's priority,

I wish I didn't know the feeling of the word that is lonely...

You cannot understand,

I forgot my flaws,

When I saw your glimpse on moon,

It brought tears to my eyes,

When I saw the constellation of your name in the sky...

Soul on Fire

In every passing hour,

every relentless second, your memory haunts me relentlessly,

With each breath, every heartbeat, it's

an agonizing reminder of what can never be,

My steps are heavy with the weight of your absence,

a constant torment,

In love, they say there are no guarantees,

it's a truth I've painfully learned,

You may never love me, and yet,

I remain ensnared by this unrequited affection,

My love for you never vanishes,

One day I will meet you in real even whatever it takes,

To meet you I can die or cross millions of lakes,

In this silence, I just sit with myself,

Nights are empty,

My heart is heavy,

A soul burning with fire,

You said you will stay forever 'liar'

Every thought is about you,

Without reason I'm just craving for you,

Is it my bad luck or my faith?

Why I don't have to say those words,

Why I'm unable to stop you,

It's just the question,

Which only you solve,

If you remove the distance ...

Never fake care to somebody, we do not

know when we will hurt them…

STARS

Constellation of stars,

I can see you from far,

The point of my pen broke,

As I yearned to compose words anew,

Unveiling tales beyond your cosmic allure.

Lying beneath the stars, gazing at the lunar,

I'm afraid I won't be able to see your face,

When I'm in my grave, will you show up at my funeral?

I can see your echoes in my dreams,

But the truth is, they're just illusions.

How will I ever behold your visage as I lie in my grave?

When you come to visit, I'll be helpless, unable to gaze,

I will be helpless and unable to see your face,

In my final rest, this longing I'll forever engrave.

Still lying beneath, the stars,

Waiting for the moon, I mean you,

Feeling your presence,

Which wraps around the air,

How can I breathe when I don't want you to leave?

I can die even as I breathe,

How will I rest, how will I get you, my moon?

Take me to the night when we met,

Let's rest and meet again,

join me under the stars, let's

watch the Constellation,

Come to me from the stars and we would lay on the grass…

BRIDGE

Standing on the bridge,

Feeling blind to cross it,

Heart is cold like it stores in fridge,

Searching for love's echo, a distant whisper

, Lonely steps falter, memories start to wither,

What's next to the bridge? ,

Is it darkness or the love which I missed,

Absence in my heart,

Don't know where to start,

Love is a mess,

How to cross this painful path if I can't take one step?

Anxiety hunting on every single breath,

Hope is hopeless,

Feelings are feeling less,

My heart is a wreck,

Lost in the currents of time,

a heartache I can't outrun

Still rhymes are perfect,

The shadow of you,

A bond unbroken, I'll never forget....

CRUEL WORLD

Everyone is laughing around,

I'm the one who sitting by my own,

Uncomfortable feelings cruel world,

Only screaming   I heard,

"I have kept the chair next to me empty only for you,

waiting for you to come and spend time with me,

If every universe, in my life,

I only chose you,

Even if you hurt me again and again,

But I still fall for you the same,

Changes in seasons,

Sitting and hearing sounds of ocean,

My heart is colder, which

once was a warm embrace,

I heard the train for the distance,

Coming to bring me to my destination,

Where our memories belong,

Forever etched, a love I'll never let go...

I wish I could be the poem or part of someone's story

LOVE OR DREAM

Is it love? Or just a dream,

Your text come, so the nightmare begins to end,

You are the mayor of my heart,

You are just like an antique art,

Which I want, to God which I ask,

Everything is second but you are the first I choose,

Will you let the distance between us reduce?

I forget the world when I heard your footsteps,

If it's love why you are not mine,

If you don't care, but I saw the shine in your eyes,

You mixed in my blood cells, that's

why without you it feels like I'm in hell,

Just learning the meaning of living,

Just under your shadow,

Just trying to find you while looking inside my heart...

PLAYLIST

I still listen our old playlist,

Any temple I go,

To God only your picture I always show,

Who am I to you?

I don't know,

Trying to find my answers,

But I don't know the right place

Trying to know about what is love,

But don't know whom I should ask,

that's a hard task,

In another universe maybe I'm happy,

But why it's not in this one,

What if in every world I'm miserable,

What if in every world I'm just a loser,

What if in every universe you left me apart,

I wish I was dead,

In the coffin rather than your memories

I wish I would take a picture of you instead,

It's just you I want to see in the last 7 minutes when my body leaves my soul,

What should I tell you more?

For you should I rip my heart?

Until I'm alive it's just because of you,

Even if I died I would still see you from heaven,

Just give me your pictures in my coffin,

Little space in your heart is okay for me,

Just your face in every step I see,

all I just see.

Part of Your Story

You didn't leave,

I just let you go,

Even if you don't love,

But only love for you all I can show,

I'm just drowning in the sorrow,

Just pretending that you were my sweet dream,

Which I cannot dream for the one more time,

I'm throwing rock at the window,

Let the wind take me to you from my hopes,

I'm empathic bard not a poet,

I shed no tears from my eyes' veil,

For my weeping flows in words' travail,

Maybe I'm close to the God,

Tearing my heart with pen which is shaped of sword,

Close to the divine I trod,

Heart torn by pen, a sword shaped by God,

Today I'm yours but in the future I wouldn't love myself,

Just going to leave myself and let destiny take the lead,

Let the pain of my heart heal my thoughts bleeds,

At the end of this universe what if I'm not there,

Not in other places but in your thoughts,

Not in myself but in your heart,

I just want to the part of your story,

Even I let you go,

Still You are my every thought...

Ink of My Tears

Feeling sad, no one can do anything,

Want to help?

Just ripped my heart and buried it in the garden,

So flowers will grow there, which going to spread love,

Don't ask me how I am,

I just smile and you would never understand,

Every line I write with the ink of my tears,

I just gave my address to the pain,

My heart aches whenever I think about why my love is just failed,

Darkness drowning in the lava, that move isn't the smartest,

The haunting shadows filled my body,

Lifting my body to the air, my soul is craving to feel the pain with no fear,

You were my moon, I was the closest star,

You were my universe, it just I was just a black dot,

You were the title of my book, I was just a line in your story,

Left me after filled with love, holds me when I needed the love,

If you ever come,

Don't ask me how I'm doing,

Don't ask me how I'm feeling,

Don't ask me what I'm dreaming,

Because my heart is drowned, my voice

shuttered in the dark, echoes from inside,

Nothing to do, just writing poetry while thinking of you....

Asymptotes of Love

The more I want to be close with someone,

The more far they go,

Just like parallel lines we never meet,

Just like a secant, we only met once in my dream,

Just like asymptotes, I am getting close to you, but unable to touch,

You are the whole tree, I'm just a branch,

The emotions are vertex,

If they fall down, it will be dead end,

Whenever you walk in the crowd, I want to be your umbra,

In the rain let me be your umbrella,

In your absence, I'm just umbra,

If you want to see your face, I be your mirror,

I be the layer of your heart, that keeps you warm....

Picture

The smile on your face,
Let my heart feel the wave,

Home is empty just your pictures on the floor,

It's midnight, in my room no light and just emptiness ,

You are the mixture of all butterflies colors,

Just mix it with my thoughts and never go away,

Sometimes my tongue slips, and your name falls where it shouldn't be,

In the dark your glimpse I see but it shouldn't be,

Roses you are atmospheric, thinking of you feels like nostalgic,

Feels so untouched in the night,

Just your pictures around where you smile,

Should I stop or keep searching for you?

Should I sleep and dream about you?

Digging a hole for my thoughts, now stuck inside it,

Just your pictures are around,

Surrounded by your memories, nothing but giving me anxiety,

In the beginning of our distance i felt broken,

Now just writing your name on the stone,

I'm thinking and sinking just feeling about you,

"I'm still alive, but your absence rips my heart twice,

Facing strobe lights feeling little warm from inside,

Let me tell you the secret, your profile picture I stare all night just all night.....

Wondering or curious

I'm wondering why I couldn't sleep at night,

Why does my chest feel so tight,

I tried to stop the time so I can esca from this feeling,

Thinking about that I'm now healing,

But I still write about you,

I still miss you ,

My heart is burning without fire,

I'm thirsty while drowning in the ocean,

The sky goes dark,

Beginning of glowing my scars,

Your memory's keep rolling with the wind,

The lighting turned into your first letter of name,

Rain drops not falling on me,

Because I have the umbrella made of pain,

Far from the stars I'm imaging you and me,

Floating in the space,

If I had power I would make a other World for you,

If I had power I would write u and I together,

I don't need your pictures, closing my eyes is enough,

You are my sky, you are the soil,

You're the heart and my soul,

Finding you in my dreams,

But it's my cursed ruined my dreams shifted into nightmares,

Promises are thing from which I only fear...

Its end guys, thanks for reading and giving my words bit time ,at last I want to say that in this generation real love is rare so just take a chance and express your real feelings.

My Instagram poetry page -- @poezio_verso The last thing I want to tell you is that no matter how hard days are, one day you going to be alright just believe in yourself…….

We are far away but am I going far from you or am I coming more close to you,

I do not know,

I do not know.

Bye(see you again)

www.ingramcontent.com/pod-product-compliance
Lightning Source LLC
Chambersburg PA
CBHW040909130726
48005CB00019BA/3036